I Can Read!

Ranger Rick

I Wish I Was a Wolf

by Jennifer Bové

HARPER
An Imprint of HarperCollinsPublishers

What if you wished you were a wolf?

Then you became a wolf pup.

Could you play like a pup?

Talk with howls and growls?

Grow up in a wolf family?

And would you want to? Find out!

Where would you live?

Wolves live all over
the northern part of the world.
They can be found in forests,
grasslands, and mountains.
They even live in the cold Arctic,
near the North Pole.

Would you like to
live here?

Wolves look like big dogs.

They act like dogs, too.

That's because they are dogs:

wild dogs.

Wolves don't live in houses.

Wolves live far from people

with their own wolf families.

What would your family be like?

A wolf family is called a pack.
The pack has a mother, a father,
and wolf kids, called pups.

Young adults help take care of
their little brothers and sisters.

A big brother or sister plays with the young pups and watches for danger while the rest of the pack goes hunting for food.

How would you learn to be a wolf?

Wolf pups watch adult wolves
and copy what they do.
Pups practice hunting
by playing with each other.
They chase and wrestle.
They will use these skills
to hunt animals for food.

How do you practice
being a grown-up?

What would you eat?

Wolves eat meat from deer, elk, caribou, moose, and bison. Wolf packs work together to hunt these large animals.

Adult wolves eat lots of meat.
Then the adults throw up mushy meat
for the young pups to eat.
Thrown-up meat is easy for pups
to chew with their little teeth.

Would you want to eat mushy meat?

How would you wash up?

Like all dogs, wolves wash up
by licking their own fur.
Mother wolves lick their pups
until they are big enough
to bathe themselves.

How would you talk?

When wolves have something to say

they lift their noses and HOWL!

A wolf pack howls together to say,

"We're a great team!"

When wolves are apart

they howl to tell others,

"I'm over here!"

Howls can be heard for many miles.

Wolves make other sounds, too.

A bark means, "Watch out!"

Whimpering means,

"Let's be friends."

Adult wolves growl to say,

"Back off!"

But pups growl for fun

when they play.

Wolves talk with their bodies, too.

A wolf shows its teeth to say,

"Leave me alone."

Wolves say hi by wagging tails,

sniffing, and rolling upside down.

How would growing up change you?

Pups begin hunting with the pack
when they are six months old.
By age three, wolves are full grown.

When they grow up,
many wolves leave their parents
to find mates from other packs.
These wolves start new packs
with pups of their own.

Would you like to grow up that fast?

Being a wolf could be cool

for a while.

But do you want to live outdoors?

Lick yourself clean?

Eat thrown-up meat?

Luckily, you don't have to.

You're not a wolf.

You're YOU!

Did You Know?

🐾 A large adult wolf can weigh up to 175 pounds (79 kilograms).

🐾 A wolf's fur can be gray, but it can also be black, white, or brown.

🐾 Wolf howls can be heard from 10 miles (16 kilometers) away.

🐾 Wolves can run as fast as 40 miles (64 kilometers) per hour.

🐾 The average life span of a wolf in the wild is six to eight years.

Fun Zone

Wolves make many sounds to talk to each other.
Their sounds have different meanings, almost like human words. Can you talk like a wolf?
Try this activity with a friend—or a whole pack of friends—to find out.

Listen to real wolf sounds on this website: www.livingwithwolves.org/about-wolves/language/#vocal

Practice making these wolf sounds:
- **Howl**
- **Growl**
- **Whimper**
- **Bark**

Try talking to friends with these sounds. Can you understand each other?

Now that you and your pack can talk like wolves, try playing a game of tag or hide-and-seek using only wolf sounds.

Wild Words

Arctic: land near the North Pole that is cold, dry, and snowy most of the year

Howl: a loud, long call made by wolves to talk over long distances

Hunt: to chase and catch animals to eat

Pack: a family of wolves

Pup: a young wolf

Dig Deeper
WANT TO FIND OUT EVEN MORE ABOUT WOLVES?

Check out the Ranger Rick website: www.RangerRick.com
SEARCH: wolves